Contents

Introduction 3
Guide to your A Level Paper 3 exam (Issues and options in psychology) 4
How to use this Exam Workbook 5
Types of A Level exam question 6
The way your answers are marked 7

Chapter 1 – Gender 8
Sex-role stereotypes and androgyny 8
The role of chromosomes and hormones in sex and gender 11
Cognitive explanations of gender development: Kohlberg's theory 14
Cognitive explanations of gender development: Gender schema theory 17
Psychodynamic explanations of gender development 20
Social learning theory as applied to gender development 23
Cultural and media influences on gender roles 26
Atypical gender development 29

Chapter 2 – Issues and debates 32
Gender in psychology: Gender bias 32
Culture in psychology: Cultural bias 35
Free will and determinism 38
The nature–nurture debate 42
Holism and reductionism 45
Idiographic and nomothetic approaches to psychological investigation 48
Ethical implications of research studies and theory 52

Introduction

The Complete Companions series of psychology textbooks were originally devised to provide everything that students would need to do well in their exams. Having produced *The Complete Companion Student Books*, the *Mini Companions*, and the *Revision and Exam Companions*, the next logical step was to produce a series of *Exam Workbooks* to provide a more hands-on experience for psychology students throughout their course and particularly in the period leading up to the exam.

Each of the *Exam Workbooks* in this series is focused on one particular exam. This book covers the topic of Gender (Paper 3: Section B) in Chapter 1 and Issues and Debates (Paper 3: Section A) in Chapter 2. Each two-page spread of psychology in the Student Book has an equivalent set of exam questions and advice in this Exam Workbook. It is designed for you to write in, so that you gain valuable experience of constructing responses to a range of different exam questions.

A distinctive feature of this *Exam Workbook* is the 'scaffolding' that we provide to help you produce effective exam answers. The concept of scaffolding is borrowed from the field of developmental psychology, where it is a metaphor describing the role of more knowledgeable individuals in guiding children's learning and development. Our scaffolding takes the form of providing sentence starters and exam tips for most questions, to help you develop the skill of writing effective exam answers. All of the material used in our scaffolding comes from the Student Book, and you are provided with page references for that book so that you can find the right material to complete the answer.

Guide to your A Level Paper 3 exam (Issues and options in psychology)

This paper contains four sections, each worth 24 marks. Section A is compulsory. For Sections B–D, you choose one topic (e.g. for Section D you choose either Aggression or Forensic Psychology or Addiction) and answer all the questions on that particular topic.

The content of the four sections is as below:

Section A
Issues and debates in psychology

All questions in this section are compulsory. Questions may focus on any of the Issues detailed in the specification (e.g. gender and cultural bias, ethical issues) or Debates (e.g. free will and determinism, the nature-nurture debate, holism and reductionism). There will be a mixture of low (e.g. 1, 2, 3 marks) and high tariff (e.g. 8, 16) marks and also a mixture of AO1 (selection, description), AO2 (application) and AO3 (evaluation) questions. Not all topics will appear in the exam but you need to revise them all as they are all equally likely to appear. You can draw on any part of the A Level specification when answering these questions, although we have restricted our focus to the topic of Gender for our material in this book.

Section B
Relationships; Gender; Cognition and development

You (or more probably your teacher) will have chosen one of these topics to study. Questions can be set on any of the different aspects of these topics that are detailed in the specification (e.g. for 'Gender', questions might focus on measuring androgyny, including the Bem Sex Role Inventory, psychodynamic explanations of gender development, gender dysphoria etc.). There will be a mix of low and high tariff marks and a mixture of AO1, AO2 and AO3 questions.

Section C
Schizophrenia; Eating behaviour; Stress

In this Section, you will have chosen to study schizophrenia eating behaviour or stress. Questions can be set on any of the different aspects of these topics that are detailed in the specification (for 'Schizophrenia', e.g. questions might focus on the classification of schizophrenia, biological and psychological explanations, token economies in the treatment of schizophrenia etc.). As with Sections A and B, there will be a mix of low and high tariff marks and a mixture of AO1, AO2 and AO3 questions.

Section D
Aggression; Forensic psychology; Addiction

As with Sections B and C, you will have chosen one of these topics to study. Again, there will be a mix of low and high tariff marks and a mixture of AO1, AO2 and AO3 questions.

The total mark for this paper will be 96 marks and you will have two hours to answer four questions (one from each Section).

How to use this Exam Workbook

Specification notes
Each spread begins with the AQA specification entry for this particular topic. This tells you what you need to learn and drives the questions that might be asked in your exam.

Student Book page reference
Each spread has a reminder of the pages where you can read about this topic in **The Complete Companion Year 2 Student Book**.

Topic links
Sometimes you will find a link between the topic on a particular spread to something in the Student Book that we feel will enhance your understanding of that topic. This might be a further discussion of the topic itself, the methods used in its investigation, or anything else that we feel might be useful to develop your understanding of that topic.

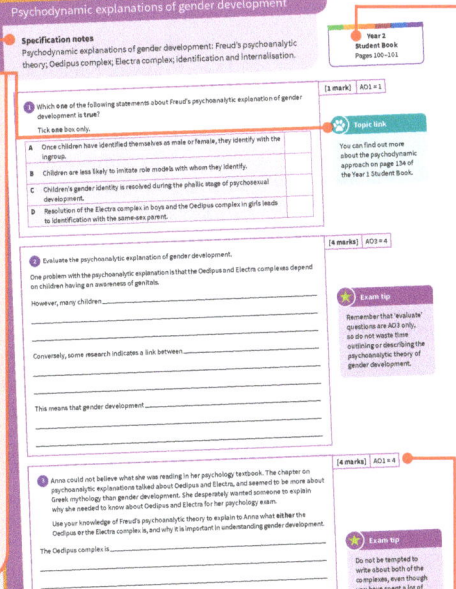

Questions
On each spread we have given you some sample exam questions. These give you experience of questions related to a particular topic area. This is not an exhaustive list of all the possible questions you could be asked on this topic, but it gives you the opportunity to practise answering the most common form of questions.

Mark box
Exam questions have different mark 'tariffs', suggesting how much you should write in response. We have tried to help you with this by giving you an appropriate number of lines in which you can fit your answer. Questions may also be AO1 (description), AO2 (application), or AO3 (evaluation), which will indicate what particular approach you should take in your response.

Scaffolding
A key feature of this Exam Workbook is that for most questions we have provided some 'scaffolding' to help you construct an effective response to the question. This scaffolding takes the form of sentence starters or appropriate links between points. You can then flesh out this material to make a full answer.

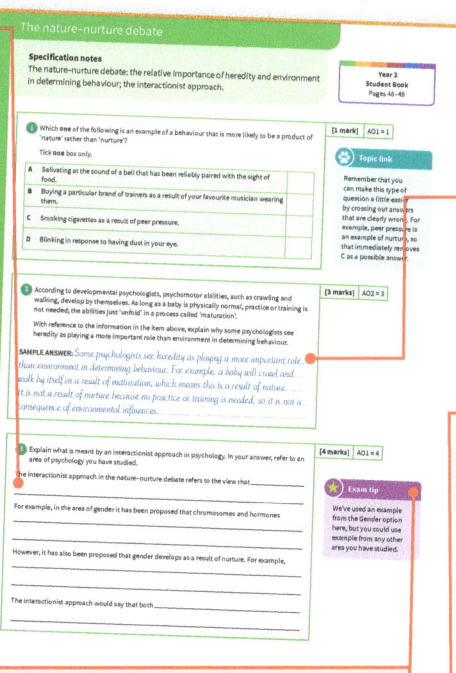

Sample answers
In some topics you will find an answer already provided. We have provided complete answers to some questions to give you some idea of the appropriate level and length of response necessary to gain full marks.

Exam tips
There are a number of helpful exam tips throughout the Exam Workbook. Sometimes these are general pieces of advice (e.g. the importance of elaborating AO3 points for maximum impact). At other times they are specific guidance about how to answer a particular question, or how to avoid common mistakes when answering that question.

Essay question
We have included scaffolding for the AO1 and AO3 components of the 16 mark essay questions. We have usually included five AO3 points, although you may choose to use four of these in greater detail.

Types of A Level exam question

Question type	Example	Advice
Simple selection/ recognition	*Which* **one** *of the following does not form a category in the original version of Bem's Sex Role Inventory?* (1 mark) A *A high masculine and low feminine score.* B *A high ratio of masculine to feminine traits.* C *A low masculine and low feminine score.* D *A low masculine and high feminine score.*	Questions such as these should be straightforward enough, so the trick is making sure you have selected the right answer to gain maximum marks. If you aren't sure which answer is the right one, try crossing through those that are obviously wrong, thus narrowing down your options. Note also that sometimes (as here), the question requires you to identify which statement is incorrect (e.g. does **not** form), so careful reading is vital.
Description questions (e.g. Describe, Outline, Identify, and Name)	*Describe Turner's syndrome.* (4 marks) *Outline Kohlberg's three stages of gender development.* (6 marks) *Explain what is meant by an interactionist approach in psychology. In your answer, refer to an area of psychology you have studied.* (4 marks)	To judge how much to write in response to a question, simply look at the number of marks available and allow about 25 words per mark. If the sole command word is 'Name' or 'Identify', there is no need to develop a 25 word per mark response, simply identifying or naming (as required by the question) is enough.
Differences/Distinguish between	*Distinguish between Kleinefelter's syndrome and Turner's syndrome.* (3 marks) *'Some psychologists believe that phobias are acquired exclusively through classical conditioning. However, others believe that phobias are a result of genetic factors.'* *Using information in the item above, explain the difference between biological determinism and environmental determinism.* (3 marks)	You might be tempted to ignore the instruction to 'distinguish between' and simply outline the two terms or concepts named in the question. This is not what is required, and would not gain credit. Words such as 'whereas' and 'however' are good linking words to illustrate a difference between two things.
Applying knowledge	*Mary has three children called Pete, Tom, and Steven. Pete tells her that when he grows up he might become a mummy. Tom says he's being silly, and that a person can't change their sex over time. Steven says that while boys will grow into men, a man who wears a dress will become a woman.* *Use your knowledge of Kohlberg's theory to identify the stages of gender development shown by Pete, Tom, and Steven, and suggest how old Steven is likely to be.* (4 marks)	In these AO2 questions, you will be provided with a scenario (the question 'stem') and asked to use your psychological knowledge to provide an informed answer. You must make sure that your answer contains not only appropriate psychological content, but that this is set explicitly within the context outlined in the question stem.
Research methods questions	You will be given a description of a study and then a number of short questions such as: (a) *Identify the dependent variable in this study.* (1 mark) (b) *Was the researcher's hypothesis directional or non-directional? Explain your answer.* (2 marks) (c) *Name an appropriate statistical test that could be used to analyse the findings in this study. Give two reasons why it would be a suitable test to use.* (3 marks)	Most (but not all) research methods questions are set within the context of a hypothetical research study. This means that your answers must also be set within the context of that study. If you don't set your answers within the specific context of the study, you cannot receive full marks.
Maths questions	(a) *The psychologist decided to use the sign test. Calculate the value of 's' in this study, and explain how you arrived at this value.* (2 marks) (b) *What conclusions could the psychologists draw from the data in the table above? Refer to the mean and standard deviation values in your answer.* (4 marks)	'Maths' questions can appear anywhere on the paper, and can assess your ability to carry out simple calculations, construct graphs, and interpret data, e.g. in the first question, a correct answer and an explanation of how you arrived at this number are necessary for maximum marks.
Evaluation questions	*Evaluate gender schema theory.* (4 marks) *Briefly evaluate the nomothetic approach to psychological investigation.* (4 marks)	It is important that you elaborate your evaluative points for maximum marks. We have shown you how to achieve this through the 'scaffolding' feature.
Mixed description and evaluation questions	*Briefly outline and evaluate gender schema theory.* (6 marks) *Briefly explain what is meant by biological and environmental reductionism and give* **one** *limitation of reductionist explanations of behaviour.* (6 marks)	Not all questions are straightforward 'description only' or 'evaluation only', but may be mixed. As a rule of thumb, in questions like these you should divide your AO1 and AO3 content equally.
Extended writing questions	*Outline and evaluate the concept of androgyny. Refer to Bem's Sex Role Inventory in your answer.* (12 marks) *Discuss the influence of culture* **and/or** *media on gender roles into media influences on aggression.* (16 marks) *Discuss the issue of cultural bias in psychological research.* (16 marks)	As a rough guide, 300-360 words would be appropriate for an answer to a 12-mark question and 400-500 words for a 16-mark question. As there are more marks allocated to AO3 than AO1, then your response should contain more AO3 than AO1 content. If the command word is 'Discuss', you should go a bit deeper in your AO3, possibly looking at both sides of an argument or considering the implications or applications of the topic being discussed.

The way your answers are marked

Questions and mark schemes

Examiners mark your answers using mark schemes and marking criteria. These vary from question to question, depending on the specific demands, but below are some examples.

1-mark questions: 1 mark is given for an accurate selection of the right answer or an appropriate identification. Giving the wrong answer or selecting more than one alternative from those available would result in 0 marks.

2-mark questions: For questions such as *'Explain what is meant by "no significant difference between the two groups at the 5% significance level"'*, and *'Give one disadvantage of using the mean as a measure of central tendency'*, a little elaboration is necessary to push your answer up from 1 mark to 2 marks. Other 2-mark questions such as *'Calculate the mean score from this data, and show your calculations'* have two requirements (i.e. the correct answer and appropriate workings), which would receive 1 mark each.

3-mark questions: These questions might focus on a descriptive point, e.g. *'Briefly explain the issue of cultural relativism in psychology'*, where the mark awarded would reflect the detail, accuracy, and overall organisation of your answer. They can also be evaluative, e.g. *'Give one limitation of the nomothetic approach to psychological investigation'*. The number of marks awarded in these AO3 questions is largely determined by the degree of elaboration of your critical point.

4-mark questions: Descriptive and evaluative questions can sometimes be assigned 4 marks, so will require slightly more detail or elaboration than you would write for a 3-mark question. It is useful to try to write the same number of 'points' as the marks available. You may be familiar with the PEEL (Point, Evidence, Explanation, Link) approach that involves making four different statements for a 4-mark AO3 question. Sometimes 4-mark questions are simply two 2-mark questions in disguise, i.e. they contain two specific components, each worth 2 marks.

6-mark questions: These can have very different requirements (e.g. description only, description plus application, or evaluation only), in which case their actual wording varies, e.g. you may come across a question such as *'Describe how social learning theory explains gender development'* (6 marks) or *'Briefly outline and evaluate the idiographic approach to psychological investigation'* (6 marks). For each of these you need to decide what is an appropriate level of breadth (e.g. how many descriptive points for each of these questions, how many evaluative points for the second question) and depth (how much detail, how much elaboration).

8-, 12-, and 16-mark questions: Questions above 6 marks are generally referred to as 'extended writing' questions. They always have more than one requirement, so examiners will be assessing (usually) both AO1 and AO3 in what is effectively a short essay response. There are four main criteria that an examiner will be looking for in extended writing answers.

Description (AO1) – have you described the material accurately and added appropriate detail? There are a number of ways in which you can add detail. These include expanding your description by going a bit deeper (i.e. giving more information rather than offering a superficial overview), providing an appropriate example to illustrate the point being made, or adding a study (which adds authority and evidence of wider reading).

Discussion/Evaluation (AO3) – have you used your critical points effectively? Examiners will be assessing whether you have made the most of a critical point. A simple way is to identify the point (e.g. that there is research support), justify the point (e.g. provide the findings that back up your claim) and elaborate the point (e.g. link back to the thing being evaluated, demonstrate how research support strengthens a theory or adds support to a research study). In this Exam Workbook we have aimed at writing 30 words of evaluation per mark available for AO3.

- A Level 8-mark question = up to 5 marks for AO3 and so around 150 words of evaluation or 3 marks for AO3, if there are marks awarded for AO2, and so around 90 words for AO3
- 12-mark question = 6 marks for AO3 and so 180 words of evaluation
- 16-mark question = we have worked on the assumption that you would use five AO3 points of 60 words each. However, you might decide to just use four of the AO3 points we provide and expand each to 75 words. This is entirely appropriate.

Remember, if the command word is *'Discuss'* rather than *'Outline and evaluate',* your AO3 should be more discursive in nature. This might involve looking at both sides of an argument, considering the consequences of a particular critical point and so on.

Organisation – does your answer flow and are your arguments clear and presented in a logical manner? This is where planning pays off as you can organise a structure to your answer before you start writing. This is always more effective than just sticking stuff down as it occurs to you!

Specialist terminology – have you used the right psychological terms (giving evidence that you have actually understood what you have read or been taught) rather than presented your material in lay (i.e. non-specialist) language? This does not mean you have to write in an overly formal manner. Students often mistakenly believe that they have to use the sorts of words that they would never use in everyday life!

How do examiners work out the right mark for an answer?

Mark schemes are broken down into different levels. Each of these levels has a descriptor, which describes what an answer for that level should look like, i.e. an average performance for that range of marks. Lower levels have less demanding descriptors, and frequently make use of criteria such as 'lacking detail', 'many inaccuracies', and 'poorly organised'. Examiners must first decide on the right level for your response. To do this, they start at the lowest level to see whether the answer meets (or exceeds) the descriptor for that level. If it meets the criteria for the lowest level, the examiner moves up to the next level, and so on, until they have a match between the level descriptor and the answer.

Answers

All answers for this Exam Workbook can be found at:

www.oxfordsecondary.co.uk/completecompanionsanswers

Chapter 1 – Gender

Sex-role stereotypes and androgyny

Specification notes
Sex and gender. Sex-role stereotypes. Androgyny and measuring androgyny, including the Bem Sex Role Inventory.

Year 2 Student Book Pages 92–93

1 Which **one** of the following does **not** form a category in the original version of Bem's Sex Role Inventory?

Tick **one** box only.

A	A high masculine and low feminine score.	
B	A high ratio of masculine to feminine traits.	
C	A low masculine and low feminine score.	
D	A low masculine and high feminine score.	

[1 mark] AO1 = 1

2 Briefly evaluate the Bem Sex Role Inventory.

One strength of the Bem Sex Role Inventory is that it has high reliability. For example, _____
_____
_____
However, one limitation of the Bem Sex Role Inventory is that it may not be a valid test. For example,
_____
_____

[4 marks] AO3 = 4

 **Exam tip**

A single elaborated evaluative point can earn full marks on this question. Alternatively, you could offer two evaluative points in less detail, as has been done here.

3 A researcher used the Bem Sex Role Inventory to identify participants as androgynous or masculine. Ten androgynous and ten masculine participants were given five minutes to complete as many problem-solving exercises as they could. The researcher predicted that more problems would be solved correctly by the androgynous participants. However, the outcome of a statistical test indicated that there was no significant difference between the two groups (p>0.05).

3(a) [1 mark] AO2 = 1
3(b) [2 marks] AO2 = 2
3(c) [3 marks] AO2 = 3

(a) Identify the dependent variable in this study.
_____

(b) Was the researcher's hypothesis directional or non-directional? Explain your answer.
_____
_____
_____

 Exam tip

Research methods can be assessed in all your examinations, so be prepared for these kinds of questions to pop up anywhere!

(c) Name an appropriate statistical test that could be used to analyse the findings in this study. Give **two** reasons why it would be a suitable test to use.
_____
_____
_____
_____

(d) The researcher found that there was no significant difference between the two groups at the 5% significance level. Explain what is meant by 'no significant difference between the two groups at the 5% significance level'.

_____

_____

_____

4 Outline and evaluate the concept of androgyny. Refer to Bem's Sex Role Inventory in your answer.

[12 marks] AO1 = 6 AO3 = 6
[16 marks] AO1 = 6 AO3 = 10

The suggested paragraph starters below will help form your answer:

- Androgyny is… (AO1)
- Bem's Sex Role Inventory involves… (AO1)
- Individuals are scored by… (AO1)
- Individuals are categorised as… (AO1)
- One strength of the idea of sex-role stereotypes is that there is research support for it. For example, Smith and Lloyd… (AO3)
- One strength of research into androgyny is that there are real-world applications. For example… (AO3)
- Another strength of this research is that there is a link between androgyny and psychological health. For example, Prakesh *et al*…. (AO3)
- One strength of the Sex Role Inventory is that it is highly reliable. For example… (AO3)
- However, one limitation of the Sex Role Inventory is that its validity has been questioned. For example, Hoffman and Borders… (AO3)

> ⭐ **Exam tip**
>
> This question asks you to make reference to Bem's Sex Role Inventory in your answer. You can't receive full marks on this question if you don't do this.

The role of chromosomes and hormones in sex and gender

Specification notes
The role of chromosomes and hormones (testosterone, oestrogen and oxytocin) in sex and gender. Atypical sex chromosome patterns: Klinefelter's syndrome and Turner's syndrome.

Year 2 Student Book Pages 94–95

---

1 Which **one** of the following is a feature of Klinefelter's syndrome?

Tick **one** box only.

A	Increased levels of testosterone.	
B	An XXY chromosomal configuration.	
C	Increased levels of oestrogen.	
D	An XYY chromosomal configuration.	

[1 mark] AO1 = 1

> ★ **Exam tip**
>
> You need to know about Klinefelter's and Turner's syndrome. Don't get their features the wrong way round!

---

2 Describe Turner's syndrome.

People born with Turner's syndrome have _____

_____

This means that they are missing _____

_____

They have a vagina and a womb, but _____

_____

In terms of physical appearance, they _____

_____

[4 marks] AO1 = 4

---

3 A student was reading about a study in which male and female rats were given hormones associated with the other sex, during their early development. The effects that occurred as a result of this were unchangeable.

Identify the hormones given to the male and female rats in this study, and outline **one** way in which the behaviour of the female rats given the male hormones would have differed from female rats not given the male hormones.

The male rat was given _____

_____

The female rat was given _____

_____

One way in which the female rats' behaviour would have differed is _____

_____

[4 marks] AO2 = 4

> ★ **Exam tip**
>
> The specification names testosterone, oestrogen, and oxytocin as the hormones you need to know about.

11

4 Outline and evaluate the role of chromosomes **and** hormones in sex and gender.

| [12 marks] | AO1 = 6 | AO3 = 6 |
| [16 marks] | AO1 = 6 | AO3 = 10 |

The suggested paragraph starters below will help form your answer:

- There are several biological explanations of gender development. Genetic transmissions explain how people acquire… (AO1)
- The sex chromosomes… (AO1)
- Girls exposed to relatively large amounts of testosterone later show… (AO1)
- Genetic males will develop as females if… (AO1)
- One strength of biological explanations of gender development is that there is research support for them. For example, Reiner and Gearhart… (AO3)
- Another strength of biological explanations for gender development is that there are real-world applications of the research. For example… (AO3)
- A third strength of biological explanations is that testosterone has been shown to affect gender development in non-humans. For example, Quadagno *et al.*… (AO3)
- However, one limitation of biological explanations of gender development is that they ignore the role of culture. For example… (AO3)
- A second limitation of biological explanations for gender development is that experience, personal qualities, and socialisation (nurture) also play a role. For example… (AO3)

> **Topic link**
>
> You can read more about the role of hormones in behaviour on page 152 of the Year 1 Student Book.

Cognitive explanations of gender development: Kohlberg's theory

Specification notes
Cognitive explanations of gender development: Kohlberg's theory; gender identity, gender stability and gender constancy.

Year 2
Student Book
Pages 96–97

1 Which **one** of the following is **not** a feature of Kohlberg's theory of gender development?

Tick **one** box only.

A	Gender development occurs in stages.	
B	Progression from one stage to another depends on education.	
C	Changes in gender thinking are the outcome of changes in cognitive capabilities.	
D	Transition from one stage to another is gradual rather than sudden.	

[1 mark] AO1 = 1

2 Outline Kohlberg's three stages of gender development.

Stage one is called _____

Children in this stage think _____
_____

Stage two is called _____

Children in this stage think _____
_____

Stage three is called _____

Children in this stage think _____
_____

[6 marks] AO1 = 6

> ★ **Exam tip**
>
> Think of this question as one that requires you to 'identify and summarise' three times.

3 Mary has three children called Pete, Tom, and Steven. Pete tells her that when he grows up he might become a mummy. Tom says he's being silly, and that a person can't change their sex over time. Steven says that while boys will grow into men, a man who wears a dress will become a woman.

Use your knowledge of Kohlberg's theory to identify the stages of gender development shown by Pete, Tom, and Steven, and suggest how old Steven is likely to be.

Pete is at the _____

Tom is at the _____

Steven is at the _____

His age is approximately _____

[4 marks] AO2 = 4

4 Discuss Kohlberg's theory of gender development.

| [12 marks] | AO1 = 6 | AO3 = 6 |
| [16 marks] | AO1 = 6 | AO3 = 10 |

The suggested paragraph starters below will help form your answer:

- Kohlberg's theory says that gender… (AO1)
- The first stage is… (AO1)
- Children at this stage think… (AO1)
- The second stage is… (AO1)
- Children at this stage think… (AO1)
- The third stage is… (AO1)
- Children at this stage think… (AO1)
- One strength of Kohlberg's theory of gender development is that there is research support for it. For example, Thompson… (AO3)
- However, one limitation of Kohlberg's theory is that there are methodological problems with the research. For example… (AO3)
- Another limitation of this theory is that children may develop gender constancy at a younger age than Kohlberg suggested. For example, Slaby and Frey… (AO3)
- A third limitation of Kohlberg's theory is that children can have gender stereotypes without gender constancy. For example, Martin and Little… (AO3)
- A final limitation with Kohlberg's theory is that social learning theory may be a better explanation of gender development. For example… (AO3)

> **Exam tip**
>
> Remember, if the command word is 'Discuss', you are expected to go beyond just stating strengths and limitations and should offer a more discursive approach to your AO3. This might include presenting the other side of an argument, considering the implications of a point or perhaps looking at how our understanding of **Kohlberg's theory** has led to applications in real life.

Cognitive explanations of gender development: Gender schema theory

Specification notes
Cognitive explanations of gender development: gender schema theory.

Year 2 Student Book
Pages 98–99

[1 mark] | AO1 = 1

1 Which **one** of the following is a feature of the gender schema theory of gender development?

Tick **one** box only.

A	The claim that gender identity leads to the development of the ability to conserve.	
B	The claim that gender-relevant information is acquired before gender constancy is achieved.	
C	The claim that gender-relevant information is acquired after gender constancy is achieved.	
D	The claim that the ability to conserve is dependent on gender constancy.	

 Topic link

You can find out more about schemas on page 130 of the Year 1 Student Book.

[4 marks] | AO3 = 4

2 Evaluate gender schema theory.

One problem with gender schema theory is that research suggests gender identity may form earlier than the theory says.

For example, Zosuls *et al.* recorded _____

_____

They found that _____

_____

This means that _____

_____

 Exam tip

As there are only 4 marks available, you can choose to make one evaluative point in more detail, or two evaluation points in less detail.

3(a) [4 marks] | AO2 = 4

3 A team of psychologists gave four-year-old girls some trucks and dolls to play with for 20 minutes. The psychologists recorded how long the girls played with each of the toys. The findings are summarised in the table below:

	Trucks	Dolls
Mean percentage of time spent playing with the toy (minutes)	2.4	16.7
Standard deviation	0.6	3.8

(a) What conclusions could the psychologists draw from the data in the table above? Refer to the mean **and** standard deviation values in your answer.

_____
_____
_____
_____
_____
_____

 Topic link

You can find out more about measures of central tendency and measures of dispersion on page 212 of the Year 1 Student Book.

17

(b) Give **one** disadvantage of using the mean as a measure of central tendency.

_____

_____

_____

(c) Suggest an alternative measure of central tendency that could have been used in this study. Explain how this alternative measure would be calculated.

_____

_____

_____

_____

3(b)	[2 marks]	AO3 = 2
3(c)	[3 marks]	AO1 = 3

Exam tip

Would the mean be a useful way of summarising a set of scores when most people got very low scores and one or two people got very high scores?

---

4 Outline and evaluate gender schema theory.

[12 marks]	AO1 = 6	AO3 = 6
[16 marks]	AO1 = 6	AO3 = 10

The suggested paragraph starters below will help form your answer:

- Schemas are… (AO1)
- Ingroup schemas are… (AO1)
- Outgroup schemas are… (AO1)
- Gender beliefs lead children to hold very fixed gender attitudes because… (AO1)
- Children believe that same-sex peers are 'like me' and therefore… (AO1)
- They also learn to avoid negative consequences of ignoring schemas, such as… (AO1)
- One strength of gender schema theory is that there is research support for it. For example, Martin and Little… (AO3)
- Another strength of this theory is that research suggests children pay greater attention to ingroup schemas. For example, Bradbard *et al.*… (AO3)
- A third strength of gender schema theory is that research supports the idea that gender schemas may distort inconsistent information to maintain ingroup schemas. For example, Martin and Halverson… (AO3)
- However, one limitation of gender schema theory is that gender stereotypes may not be entirely fixed. For example, Hoffman… (AO3)
- Another limitation of this theory is that research suggests gender identity may be earlier than gender schema theory says. For example, Zosuls *et al.*… (AO3)

Exam tip

Studies can be used as evaluation points, provided you write about why they support or challenge gender schema theory. If you don't do this, you won't receive any AO3 credit.

Psychodynamic explanations of gender development

Specification notes
Psychodynamic explanations of gender development: Freud's psychoanalytic theory; Oedipus complex; Electra complex; identification and internalisation.

> **Year 2 Student Book**
> Pages 100–101

1 Which **one** of the following statements about Freud's psychoanalytic explanation of gender development is **true**?

Tick **one** box only.

[1 mark] AO1 = 1

A	Once children have identified themselves as male or female, they identify with the ingroup.	
B	Children are less likely to imitate role models with whom they identify.	
C	Children's gender identity is resolved during the phallic stage of psychosexual development.	
D	Resolution of the Electra complex in boys and the Oedipus complex in girls leads to identification with the same-sex parent.	

Topic link

You can find out more about the psychodynamic approach on page 134 of the Year 1 Student Book.

2 Evaluate the psychoanalytic explanation of gender development.

[4 marks] AO3 = 4

One problem with the psychoanalytic explanation is that the Oedipus and Electra complexes depend on children having an awareness of genitals.

However, many children _____

_____

_____

Conversely, some research indicates a link between _____

_____

_____

This means that gender development _____

_____

_____

Exam tip

Remember that 'evaluate' questions are AO3 only, so do not waste time outlining or describing the psychoanalytic theory of gender development.

3 Anna could not believe what she was reading in her psychology textbook. The chapter on psychoanalytic explanations talked about Oedipus and Electra, and seemed to be more about Greek mythology than gender development. She desperately wanted someone to explain why she needed to know about Oedipus and Electra for her psychology exam.

Use your knowledge of Freud's psychoanalytic theory to explain to Anna what **either** the Oedipus **or** the Electra complex is, and why it is important in understanding gender development.

[4 marks] AO1 = 4

The Oedipus complex is _____

_____

_____

The complex is resolved when _____

_____

_____

Exam tip

Do not be tempted to write about both of the complexes, even though you have spent a lot of time revising them! The question says 'either/or'.

It is important in understanding gender development because _____
_____
_____

4 Outline and evaluate Freud's psychoanalytic theory of gender development.

[12 marks] AO1 = 6 AO3 = 6
[16 marks] AO1 = 6 AO3 = 10

The suggested paragraph starters below will help form your answer:

- The psychoanalytic theory says that we develop in psychosexual stages, where the libido… (AO1)
- In the phallic stage, boys develop their gender identity through the Oedipus complex. This is… (AO1)
- The complex is resolved when… (AO1)
- Girls develop their gender identity through the Electra complex. This is… (AO1)
- The complex is resolved when… (AO1)
- If the phallic stage is not resolved… (AO1)
- One strength of the psychodynamic explanation of gender development is that there is research support for it. For example, Freud's Little Hans study… (AO3)
- However, one limitation of this explanation is that there are methodological issues with case studies. For example… (AO3)
- A second limitation of the psychodynamic explanation of gender development is that the Oedipus and Electra complexes depend on children having an awareness of genitals. However… (AO3)
- A third limitation of Freud's explanation is that it does not adequately explain female gender development. For example… (AO3)
- A final limitation of Freud's explanation of gender development is that there are alternative explanations for gender development. For example, Chodorow… (AO3)

> ⭐ **Exam tip**
>
> There are lots of ways of evaluating any theory. These include research support, research challenges, methodological issues, alternative explanations, and so on.

Social learning theory as applied to gender development

Specification notes
Social learning theory as applied to gender development.

> Year 2 Student Book
> Pages 102–103

[1 mark] AO1 = 1

1 Which **one** of the following is **not** a feature of social learning theory as applied to gender development?

Tick **one** box only.

A	Indirect reinforcement.	
B	Self-direction.	
C	Direct reinforcement.	
D	Learned helplessness.	

> **Topic link**
>
> You can find out more about social learning theory on page 128 of the Year 1 Student Book.

[6 marks] AO1 = 6

2 Describe how social learning theory explains gender development.

Social learning theory says we learn by _____

Children observe the gender behaviour of others from _____

They learn whether a behaviour should be imitated by _____

Girls identify with other females and are more likely to _____

Boys may observe their mother, but are _____

This gendered behaviour is maintained by _____

> **Exam tip**
>
> Look at the way the scaffolding provided helps you to structure your answer, so that it is both sufficiently detailed and coherently organised.

3(a) [3 marks] AO2 = 3

3 A researcher was interested in the relationship between the amount of time children spend watching television and their knowledge of adult sex-role stereotypes. The researcher believed that because gender roles are commonly depicted in television programmes, a directional hypothesis could be proposed. Awareness of stereotyped sex-role perceptions held by adults was measured using the Sex Stereotype Measure, and each child's mother recorded how much television was watched over a week-long period.

(a) Write a fully operationalised directional hypothesis for the study outlined above.

_____
_____
_____
_____

(b) Name an appropriate statistical test that could be used in this study. Give **two** reasons why it would be an appropriate test to use.

_____
_____
_____
_____

(c) Outline **one** way in which the researcher could have checked the reliability of the Sex Stereotype Measure.

_____
_____
_____
_____

| 3(b) | [3 marks] | AO2 = 3 |
| 3(c) | [2 marks] | AO2 = 2 |

> ⭐ **Exam tip**
>
> Think about whether the researcher is looking for a difference or correlation, whether an experimental design has been used, and the level of measurement of the data.

---

4 Outline and evaluate social learning theory as applied to gender development.

| [12 marks] | AO1 = 6 | AO3 = 6 |
| [16 marks] | AO1 = 6 | AO3 = 10 |

The suggested paragraph starters below will help form your answer:

- Social learning theory says we learn by… (AO1)
- Children observe the gender behaviour of others from… (AO1)
- They learn whether a behaviour should be imitated by… (AO1)
- Girls identify with other females and are more likely to… (AO1)
- Boys may observe their mother, but are… (AO1)
- This gendered behaviour is maintained by… (AO1)
- One strength of social learning theory as an explanation for gender development is that there is research support for it. For example, Perry and Bussey… (AO3)
- Another strength of this explanation is that research suggests children learn to evaluate others' behaviour, and then their own. For example, Bussey and Bandura… (AO3)
- However, one limitation of social learning theory as an explanation for gender development is that direct instruction may be more effective than modelling. For example, Martin *et al.*… (AO3)
- Another limitation of this explanation is that peers may not be important in early childhood when gender is being formed. For example… (AO3)
- A final limitation of social learning theory as an explanation for gender development is that it focuses too much on social processes and ignores the role of biology. For example… (AO3)

_____
_____
_____
_____
_____
_____

Cultural and media influences on gender roles

Specification notes
The influence of culture and media on gender roles.

Year 2 Student Book Pages 104–105

---

1 Which **one** of the following has **not** been proposed as a way by which the media might influence gender roles?

Tick **one** box only.

A	Portrayal of stereotypes.	
B	Counter-stereotypes.	
C	Role models.	
D	Role conflict.	

[1 mark] AO1 = 1

---

2 Outline how culture influences gender roles.

Gender expectations vary between cultures. For example, Mead found _____
_____
_____

These expectations also change over time. For example, _____
_____
_____

[4 marks] AO1 = 4

⭐ **Exam tip**

Remember that 'Outline' questions are AO1 only, so avoid the temptation to offer any form of evaluation.

---

3 Jane and Sarah were deciding which film they were going to watch that night. Sarah said she would only watch a film that had more than two women in it, and who spoke to each other about something other than men! Jane tried hard, but said she could not think of a film like that.

Referring to Jane's comments, briefly explain how the media influences gender roles.

Bussey and Bandura found the media portrays men as _____
_____
_____

However, women are more likely to be portrayed as _____
_____
_____

This may be why Jane couldn't _____
_____
_____

[4 marks] AO1 = 2 AO2 = 2

⭐ **Exam tip**

The question asks you to use information from the item, so remember to contextualise your answer rather than writing a general explanation of how the media influences gender roles.

4 Discuss the influence of culture **and/or** media on gender roles.

[12 marks] AO1 = 6 AO3 = 6
[16 marks] AO1 = 6 AO3 = 10

The suggested paragraph starters below will help form your answer:

- Gender expectations vary between cultures. For example, Mead found… (AO1)
- These expectations also change over time. For example… (AO1)
- The media portrays men as… (AO1)
- However, women are more likely to be portrayed as… (AO1)
- The media can maintain stereotypes, but it can also change them. For example… (AO1)
- One limitation of cross-cultural research is that observers may be biased in their interpretation of behaviour. For example… (AO3)
- A problem with the idea that culture influences gender roles is that these roles may be a product of biological differences. For example, Eagly and Wood… (AO3)
- One strength of the idea that exposure to the media influences gender attitudes is that there is research support for it. For example, Williams… (AO3)
- However, one limitation of the idea that media can change expectations is that research does not always support it. For example, Pingree… (AO3)
- Another limitation of the idea that the media affects gender roles is that this effect may be insignificant. For example, Charlton *et al.*… (AO3)

Exam tip

You need to make sure that each of your evaluation points links back to the question.

Atypical gender development

Specification notes
Atypical gender development: gender dysphoria; biological and social explanations for gender dysphoria.

Year 2
Student Book
Pages 106–107

---

1 Which one of the following best describes gender dysphoria? [1 mark] AO1 = 1

Tick **one** box only.

A	A person feels their biological sex is more important than their gender identity.	
B	A person feels their biological sex might not match their gender identity.	
C	A person feels their biological sex matches their gender identity.	
D	A person feels distress because their gender identity does not match their biological sex.	

---

2 Outline **one or more** biological explanations of gender dysphoria. [4 marks] AO1 = 4

Brain-sex theory says that _____

_____

For example, the size of the bed nucleus of the stria terminalis (BSTc) correlates with _____

_____

_____

Gender dysphoria may be due to innate cross-wiring _____

_____

_____

For example, Ramachandran *et al.* _____

_____

_____

> ⭐ **Exam tip**
>
> When a question asks you for 'one or more', you can write about one biological explanation in detail, or several biological explanations in less detail.

---

3 Outline **one or more** social explanations of gender dysphoria. [4 marks] AO1 = 4

Research suggests that gender dysphoria can be a result of childhood trauma. For example,

_____

_____

_____

Research also suggests that gender dysphoria is caused by _____

_____

For example, _____

_____

_____

> ⭐ **Exam tip**
>
> On this kind of question you can adopt a 'depth' approach and write about one explanation, or a 'breadth' approach and write about more than one explanation, as we suggest here.

4 One method that has been used to study gender dysphoria in children is the Draw-a-Person test. Studies show that children with gender dysphoria tend to draw opposite-sex persons first, and to draw them in more detail compared with their drawing of the same-sex person. The test is reliable, but whether it is a valid measure of gender dysphoria has yet to be established.

4(a)	[3 marks]	AO1 = 3
4(b)	[3 marks]	AO2 = 3
4(c)	[4 marks]	AO1 = 4

(a) Distinguish between reliability and validity.

_____
_____
_____
_____

 Exam tip

Whenever you are asked to distinguish between two things, use words like 'however' or 'whereas'.

(b) Explain how the concurrent validity of the Draw-a-Person test might be assessed.

_____
_____
_____
_____
_____
_____

(c) Apart from concurrent validity, identify and briefly outline **two** other types of validity in psychological research.

_____
_____
_____
_____
_____
_____
_____
_____

 Exam tip

The specification identifies four types of validity that you must be familiar with, so choose the two you feel most comfortable outlining.

---

5 Outline and evaluate research related to gender dysphoria.

| [12 marks] | AO1 = 6 | AO3 = 6 |
| [16 marks] | AO1 = 6 | AO3 = 10 |

The suggested paragraph starters below will help form your answer:

- Research suggests there might be a transsexual gene… (AO1)
- Brain-sex theory says that… (AO1)
- Gender dysphoria may be due to innate cross-wiring… (AO1)
- Distorted parental attitudes may lead to confused gender identity… (AO1)
- Gender dysphoria may be the result of childhood trauma… (AO1)
- One strength of biological explanations of gender dysphoria is that there is research support for cross-wiring. For example, Ramachandran and McGeoch… (AO3)
- However, one problem with the brain-sex theory is that it is hard to see whether differences are an effect, or a cause, of gender dysphoria. For example, Chung *et al.*… (AO3)
- One strength of social explanations of gender dysphoria is that there is research support for them. For example, Zucker *et al.*… (AO3)

 Exam tip

'Research' can mean theories or studies, so you could choose to answer this question using either or both.

- However, one issue with trying to explain gender dysphoria is that there are two distinct groups of male to female transsexuals. For example, Furuhashi… (AO3)
- Another issue with trying to explain gender dysphoria is that it has potential social consequences for individuals with dysphoria. For example… (AO3)

Chapter 2 – Issues and debates

Gender in psychology: Gender bias

Specification notes
Gender in psychology – universality and bias. Gender bias including androcentrism, and alpha and beta bias.

Year 2 Student Book Pages 42–43

1 Which **one** of the following best describes the term 'alpha bias' in psychological research?

Tick **one** box only.

[1 mark] AO1 = 1

A	Minimising differences between men and women.	
B	Exaggerating differences between men and women.	
C	Focusing on men, and neglecting or excluding women.	
D	Focusing on women, and neglecting or excluding men.	

2 Researchers interviewed 40 men aged 35–45 from a variety of occupational backgrounds. Transcripts were made of the interviews, which took place over several months. The aim of the research was to look at how adulthood is actually experienced. Based on their findings, the researchers developed a 'life structure' theory of adulthood, dividing the life cycle into four major 'eras' that overlap in the form of 'cross-era transitions'. The findings were published in a book called *The Seasons of a Man's Life*.

2(a) [3 marks] AO1 = 2 AO2 = 1
2(b) [3 marks] AO2 = 3

(a) Using information in the item above, explain what is meant by the term 'androcentrism'.

_____
_____
_____

> ⭐ **Exam tip**
> Remember that androgens are the male sex hormones, such as testosterone. 'Centric' means in or at the centre.

(b) Using your knowledge of gender bias in psychological research, explain why the research above demonstrates a 'beta bias'.

The sample in this research is _____

However, the researchers developed a _____
_____

This is an example of beta bias because _____
_____

> ⭐ **Exam tip**
> A beta bias is the tendency to ignore or minimise differences between men and women.

3 A research team used the water level task with 62 male and 72 female students. Each student was shown a picture of the water level in a bottle of water, and a picture of the same bottle tipped to the right but without the water level shown, as illustrated below.

The students were asked to draw where the water line would be in the bottle tipped to the right. The results are shown below:

	Men	Women
Correct level drawn	54	34
Incorrect level drawn	8	38

(a) Identify the type of experiment that the researchers conducted.

_____

(b) What level of measurement was used by the researchers?

_____

(c) The researchers used a chi-squared test to analyse their results. Apart from the level of measurement they used, give **two** reasons why this was an appropriate test to use.

_____
_____
_____
_____
_____

3(a)	[1 mark]	AO2 = 1
3(b)	[1 mark]	AO2 = 1
3(c)	[2 marks]	AO2 = 2

> ⭐ **Exam tip**
>
> 'Apart from' means give two reasons other than the level of measurement!

---

4 Discuss gender bias in psychology.

[12 marks]	AO1 = 6	AO3 = 6
[16 marks]	AO1 = 6	AO3 = 10

The suggested paragraph starters below will help form your answer:

- A gender bias occurs when… (AO1)
- Psychology has tended to have an androcentric gender bias. This is… (AO1)
- Alpha bias occurs when… (AO1)
- Beta bias occurs when… (AO1)
- One way to reduce gender bias is to take a feminist approach. This agrees that there are… (AO3)
- A criticism of psychology research is that its methods are gender biased because… (AO3)
- Another way to reduce gender bias is to develop theories that emphasise the value of women. For example, Cornwell *et al.*… (AO3)
- One issue with beta bias is that it ignores important differences between genders. For example… (AO3)
- A final issue with gender research is that examples of gender bias remain unchallenged. For example, Darwin's theory… (AO3)

_____
_____
_____
_____
_____
_____
_____

> ⭐ **Exam tip**
>
> Remember, as the command word is 'Discuss', you are expected to go beyond just stating strengths and limitations and should offer a more discursive approach to your AO3. This might include presenting the other side of an argument, considering the implications of a point or perhaps looking at how our understanding of gender has led to attempts to overcome it.

Culture in psychology: Cultural bias

Specification notes
Culture in psychology – universality and bias. Cultural bias, including ethnocentrism and cultural relativism.

Year 2 Student Book Pages 44–45

---

1 Which **one** of the following terms describes the view that behaviour cannot be judged properly unless it is viewed in the context in which it originates?

Tick **one** box only.

[1 mark] AO1 = 1

A	Ethnocentrism.	
B	Cultural relativism.	
C	Universality.	
D	Cultural bias.	

---

2 Research has shown that, when infants from other cultures are raised in a new one (for example, an Asian family emigrates to the UK), within two or three generations, the children of that family will be all but indistinguishable from their 'new' cultural peers.

Explain why the item above supports the idea of 'universality'.

_____
_____
_____

[2 marks] AO2 = 2

> **Exam tip**
> This question is not asking what we mean by 'universality', but why this scenario is an example of it.

---

3 When he developed his 'line judgement' task as a way of studying conformity, Asch (1951) found that male American undergraduates conformed about 32 per cent of the time on this task. When members of other cultural groups are studied using the 'line judgement' task, they are typically compared with Asch's participants, who are described as the 'standard'.

(a) Using information in the item above, explain what is meant by the term 'ethnocentrism'.

_____
_____
_____

3(a) [3 marks] AO1 = 2 AO2 = 1
3(b) [4 marks] AO3 = 4

(b) Studies such as Asch's are often conducted in a laboratory setting. Outline **one** strength and **one** limitation of conducting research in this way.

One strength of conducting research in a laboratory is _____

This is because _____
_____

One limitation of conducting research in a laboratory is _____

This is because _____
_____

> **Exam tip**
> The question requires you to write about one strength and one limitation, rather than two of either.

4 Discuss the issue of cultural bias in psychological research.

[12 marks] AO1 = 6 AO3 = 6
[16 marks] AO1 = 6 AO3 = 10

The suggested paragraph starters below will help form your answer:

- A cultural bias is… (AO1)
- There are different types of cultural bias, including… (AO1)
- Ethnocentrism is… (AO1)
- Cultural relativism is… (AO1)
- One strength of cultural research is the development of indigenous psychologies. This is… (AO3)
- However, one issue with cultural research is the development of culturally specific theories. For example… (AO3)
- Cultural bias can be dealt with by using better, more representative, sampling methods. For example… (AO3)
- One issue that can arise from culturally biased research is the formation of stereotypes. For example… (AO3)
- One strength of psychological research today is that researchers are more culturally aware. For example… (AO3)

Exam tip

Evaluation of material can take several forms. For example, you could write about theories, studies, methodological and/or ethical issues, and so on. Remember, though, that you must show clearly why an issue you have raised should be credited as evaluation.

Free will and determinism

Specification notes
Free will and determinism: hard determinism and soft determinism; biological, environmental and psychic determinism. The scientific emphasis on causal explanations.

Year 2
Student Book
Pages 46–47

---

1 Which **one** of the following statements best describes psychic determinism?

Tick **one** box only.

A	Behaviour is determined by forces outside of the individual.	
B	Behaviour is determined by a mixture of innate drives and early experience.	
C	Behaviour is determined by instinct.	
D	Behaviour is determined by genes.	

[1 mark] AO1 = 1

 Exam tip

Psychic determinism is most closely associated with Freud's psychoanalytic theory of personality.

---

2 Stuart suffers from a rare condition called Tourette's disorder. His head sometimes jerks and he often blinks and grimaces. Occasionally, he blurts out words; usually rude words. He does not mean to do it and is embarrassed by it, but he cannot control it. Because of his strange behaviour, most other children avoid him. His isolation and embarrassment are interfering with his social development.

Using the case of Stuart, explain the difference between determinism and free will.

Determinism is _____

_____

For example, when Stuart _____

_____

However, free will is _____

_____

[3 marks] AO2 = 3

 Topic link

It is a good idea to revisit the major approaches that you studied in Book 1 (Chapter 5), particularly their stance on the free-will versus determinism debate. This will give you invaluable material when writing answers on this topic.

---

3 Some psychologists believe that phobias are acquired exclusively through classical conditioning. However, others believe that phobias are a result of genetic factors.

Using information in the item above, explain the difference between biological determinism and environmental determinism.

Biological determinism is _____

_____

For example, phobias are acquired _____

_____

However, environmental determinism is _____

_____

For example, phobias are acquired _____

_____

[3 marks] AO1 = 2 AO2 = 1

 Exam tip

The question requires you to use the information in the item (how phobias are acquired). Writing a general answer will earn you some marks, but you can only be awarded full marks if you contextualise your answer.

4. In clinical trials, researchers compare the effectiveness of an experimental drug with the effectiveness of a placebo.

   Using information in the item above, explain why causal explanations are important in scientific research.

   [3 marks] AO1 = 2 AO2 = 1

   Scientific research is based on the assumption that _____

   _____

   In experiments, an IV is manipulated in order to _____

   _____

   Causal explanations are important in scientific research because _____

   _____

5. Explain the difference between hard determinism and soft determinism.

   [3 marks] AO1 = 3

   Hard determinism is _____

   _____

   Whereas, soft determinism is _____

   _____

   Exam tip

   Remember that when you are asked to explain the difference between two things, you need to compare them. Using words such as 'whereas' or 'however' will help you.

6. Twenty students read a fictitious court case about a man charged with murder. The man's lawyer argued that his client was suffering from a serious mental disorder in which he heard voices in his head telling him to commit murder. The lawyer argued that his client could not be guilty of murder, because he was suffering from a mental disorder at the time of the offence. The students were asked to decide if they thought the man was guilty. Fifteen said he was and five said he was not.

   The students then read the case for the prosecution, whose lawyer argued that the disorder was not severe enough to stop him being responsible for the crime. The students were asked to make another decision about the man's guilt. Eight did not change their opinion about the man's guilt. However, one who had previously judged the man to be guilty changed his mind, and eleven who had previously judged the man to be not guilty changed theirs.

   6(a) [2 marks] AO1 = 2
   6(b) [2 marks] AO2 = 2

   (a) A psychologist wanted to analyse this data statistically. Explain why statistical testing is used in psychological research.

   _____

   _____

   _____

   (b) The psychologist decided to use the sign test. Calculate the value of 's' in this study, and explain how you arrived at this value.

   _____

   _____

   _____

   Exam tip

   This looks as though it is going to be a question on determinism, but instead it uses that topic to ask you about features of science and statistical tests. As we've said before, be prepared for research methods questions to pop up anywhere!

7 Outline and evaluate the free will and determinism debate in psychology.

[12 marks] AO1 = 6 AO3 = 6
[16 marks] AO1 = 6 AO3 = 10

The suggested paragraph starters below will help form your answer:

- Determinism is… (AO1)
- There are different types of determinism. Biological determinism is… (AO1)
- Environmental determinism is… (AO1)
- Psychic determinism is… (AO1)
- Free will is… (AO1)
- One issue with determinism is that no behaviour is completely environmentally determined. For example… (AO3)
- Another issue with determinism is that no behaviour is completely biologically determined. For example, twin studies… (AO3)
- A third issue with the idea of determinism is that it provides an excuse for unacceptable behaviours. For example… (AO3)
- One issue with the idea of free will is the lack of support from cognitive neuroscience. For example, Libet *et al.*… (AO3)
- Another issue with the idea of free will is that free will may just be an illusion. For example, Skinner… (AO3)

> **Exam tip**
>
> Writing about hard determinism and soft determinism would also earn you marks.

The nature–nurture debate

Specification notes
The nature–nurture debate: the relative importance of heredity and environment in determining behaviour; the interactionist approach.

Year 2
Student Book
Pages 48–49

1 Which **one** of the following is an example of a behaviour that is more likely to be a product of 'nature' rather than 'nurture'?

Tick **one** box only.

A	Salivating at the sound of a bell that has been reliably paired with the sight of food.	
B	Buying a particular brand of trainers as a result of your favourite musician wearing them.	
C	Smoking cigarettes as a result of peer pressure.	
D	Blinking in response to having dust in your eye.	

[1 mark] AO1 = 1

 Exam tip

Remember that you can make this type of question a little easier by crossing out answers that are clearly wrong. For example, peer pressure is an example of nurture, so that immediately removes C as a possible answer.

2 According to developmental psychologists, psychomotor abilities, such as crawling and walking, develop by themselves. As long as a baby is physically normal, practice or training is not needed; the abilities just 'unfold' in a process called 'maturation'.

With reference to the information in the item above, explain why some psychologists see heredity as playing a more important role than environment in determining behaviour.

SAMPLE ANSWER: *Some psychologists see heredity as playing a more important role than environment in determining behaviour. For example, a baby will crawl and walk by itself as a result of maturation, which means this is a result of nature. It is not a result of nurture because no practice or training is needed, so it is not a consequence of environmental influences.*

[3 marks] AO2 = 3

3 Explain what is meant by an interactionist approach in psychology. In your answer, refer to an area of psychology you have studied.

The interactionist approach in the nature–nurture debate refers to the view that _____

_____

For example, in the area of gender it has been proposed that chromosomes and hormones

_____

_____

However, it has also been proposed that gender develops as a result of nurture. For example,

_____

_____

The interactionist approach would say that both _____

_____

[4 marks] AO1 = 4

 Exam tip

We've used an example from the Gender option here, but you could use an example from any other area you have studied.

4 A team of psychologists studied violinists who had been learning to play their instruments since the age of five. They found that the most able violinists averaged around 10,000 hours of practice, whereas the less able averaged only 4,000 hours of practice. No 'naturally gifted' performers emerged, and there was a statistically significant positive correlation between hours of practice and achievement.

4(a)	[3 marks]	AO2 = 3
4(b)	[1 mark]	AO2 = 1
4(c)	[2 marks]	AO2 = 2
4(d)	[1 mark]	AO1 = 1

(a) Briefly explain the outcome of this study in relation to the nature–nurture debate.

_____
_____
_____
_____

(b) Suggest a way in which the psychologists could have operationalised the violinists' ability.

_____
_____

Exam tip

Remember, operationalisation means defining a variable in a way in which it can be measured.

(c) The psychologists measured how long the violinists practised using a self-report technique. Explain how demand characteristics might have occurred in this study.

_____
_____
_____

Exam tip

You only have to name a test. You have not been asked to justify your choice of test.

(d) Name a statistical test that could have been used to measure the strength of the correlation between achievement and hours of practice.

_____

5 Outline and evaluate the nature–nurture debate in psychology. Refer in your answer to **at least one** area of psychology you have studied.

| [12 marks] | AO1 = 6 | AO3 = 6 |
| [16 marks] | AO1 = 6 | AO3 = 10 |

The suggested paragraph starters below will help form your answer:

- The nature–nurture debate is… (AO1)
- Nature refers to… (AO1)
- For example, in the area of gender, it has been proposed that… (AO1)
- Nurture refers to… (AO1)
- For example, our gender is the result of… (AO1)
- One consideration in the nature-nurture debate is the idea that nature affects nurture. For example… (AO3)
- A second consideration in the nature–nurture debate is the idea that nurture affects nature. For example… (AO3)
- One strength of the nature–nurture debate is the development of the diathesis-stress model. This is… (AO3)
- Another consideration in the nature–nurture debate is the role of epigenetics. This is… (AO3)
- One issue with the nature–nurture debate is that the debate has become meaningless. This is because… (AO3)

Exam tip

The question says 'at least one area of psychology you have studied'. We've taken a 'depth' approach here and looked at only one area, rather than taking a 'breadth' approach that looks at several areas.

_____
_____

Holism and reductionism

Specification notes
Holism and reductionism: levels of explanation in psychology. Biological reductionism and environmental (stimulus–response) reductionism.

Year 2 Student Book Pages 50–51

1 Which **one** of the following statements about reductionism and holism is **false**?

Tick **one** box only.

A	Behaviourist psychologists believe that all behaviour can be explained in terms of a simple relationship between behaviour and events in the environment.	
B	Humanistic psychologists believe that individuals react as an organised whole rather than a set of stimulus–response links.	
C	Biological psychologists believe that behaviour can be reduced to the actions of things like neurons and neurotransmitters.	
D	Cognitive psychologists believe that the only way to explain behaviour is in terms of the influences exerted by cultural factors rather than biological factors.	

[1 mark] AO1 = 1

2 Using examples from areas of psychology you have studied, explain the difference between biological reductionism and environmental reductionism.

Biological reductionism is _____

_____

For example, the biological approach attempts to explain gender as being a result of _____

_____

_____

However, environmental reductionism is _____

_____

For example, the behaviourist approach attempts to explain phobias as being a result of _____

_____

_____

[4 marks] AO1 = 4

> **Exam tip**
>
> Note that the question asks for 'areas' rather than a single 'area'. We've used examples from gender and psychopathology to help you construct your answer.

3 'You, your joys and your sorrows, your memories and your ambitions, your sense of personality and free will, are in fact no more than the behaviour of a vast assembly of nerve cells and their associated molecules.' (Crick, 1994)

With reference to the quotation above, briefly evaluate biological reductionism.

One issue with biological reductionism is that it ignores the context and function of behaviour.

For example, to say that we are 'no more than the behaviour of a vast assembly of nerve cells', fails

_____

_____

This means that _____

_____

[4 marks] AO2 = 2 AO3 = 2

> **Exam tip**
>
> There is no need to give an outline of biological determinism, since the question only asks for evaluation.

4 A psychologist asked members of the public to tell her which of two statements they agreed with more strongly. The statements were:

(1) The best way to explain how memory works is in terms of how cultural expectations affect what we remember.

(2) The best way to explain how memory works is in terms of brain structures and brain chemicals.

The psychologist predicted that people would be more likely to agree with the second statement than the first.

(a) Using information in the item above, outline what psychologists mean by 'levels of explanation'.

4(a)	[3 marks]	AO1 = 2	AO2 = 1
4(b)	[1 mark]	AO2 = 1	
4(c)	[2 marks]	AO2 = 2	

⭐ **Exam tip**

Be careful! Question (a) asks about 'levels of explanation', but question (b) asks about levels of measurement.

_____
_____
_____
_____
_____

(b) What level of measurement did the psychologist use in her investigation?

_____

(c) Was the psychologist's hypothesis directional or non-directional? Explain your answer.

_____
_____
_____

---

5 Discuss reductionism in psychology.

| [12 marks] | AO1 = 6 | AO3 = 6 |
| [16 marks] | AO1 = 6 | AO3 = 10 |

The suggested paragraph starters below will help form your answer:

- A reductionist approach involves... (AO1)
- There are different types of reductionism. Biological reductionism is the view that... (AO1)
- Environmental reductionism is... (AO1)
- Experimental reductionism is... (AO1)
- A strength of biological reductionism is the development of drug therapies. For example... (AO3)
- An issue with environmental reductionism is that the experiments may not apply to human behaviour. For example... (AO3)
- An issue with experimental reductionism is that the research findings may not be applicable to everyday life. For example... (AO3)
- An issue with a reductionist approach in general is that it can lead to errors in understanding. For example... (AO3)
- It may be better to consider an interactionist point of view rather than take a reductionist approach because... (AO3)

Exam tip

When the command word is 'discuss', you are expected to go beyond just stating strengths and limitations. Introducing alternatives, such as the interactionist approach, is one way of making your answer more 'discursive'.

_____
_____

Idiographic and nomothetic approaches to psychological investigation

Specification notes
Idiographic and nomothetic approaches to psychological investigation.

Year 2
Student Book
Pages 52–53

1 Which **one** of the following statements best describes the nomothetic and idiographic approaches in psychology?

Tick **one** box only.

A	The idiographic approach favours quantitative methods in research whereas the nomothetic approach favours qualitative methods.	
B	The nomothetic approach emphasises the uniqueness of people whereas the idiographic approach seeks to formulate general laws about people.	
C	The idiographic approach focuses on individuals whereas the nomothetic approach focuses on groups.	
D	The nomothetic approach uses descriptive statistics whereas the idiographic approach uses inferential statistics.	

[1 mark]   AO1 = 1

2 Outline **two** differences between an idiographic approach to psychological investigation and a nomothetic approach to psychological investigation.

An idiographic approach to psychological investigation focuses on _____

However, a nomothetic approach to psychological investigation attempts to _____

An idiographic approach to psychological investigation uses methods such as _____

However, a nomothetic approach to psychological investigation uses _____

[4 marks]   AO1 = 4

 Exam tip

Note that you've been asked to write about two differences rather than just one.

3 Sebastian and Christina were discussing the best way to study behaviour. 'The raw data of social life are not quantitative,' said Sebastian. 'Turning life into numbers means that some of the richness and complexity is lost.' 'I agree,' said Christina. 'We end up emphasising certain aspects of a phenomenon and neglecting certain others.'

(a) Referring to the conversation between Sebastian and Christina, explain what is meant by an idiographic approach to psychological investigation.

The idiographic approach to psychological investigation focuses on _____

It collects data that is _____

This means that _____

3(a)   [3 marks]   AO1 = 2   AO2 = 1

 Exam tip

Remember to refer to the scenario in your explanation.

48

(b) Briefly evaluate the nomothetic approach to psychological investigation.

3(b) [4 marks] AO3 = 4

SAMPLE ANSWER: *One strength of the nomothetic approach is that it produces general predictions about behaviour, which the idiographic approach does not. These general predictions can be useful, for example in producing drugs to treat mental illness. It would be far too time consuming producing personal therapies for each person. The nomothetic approach helps us to make predictions about the most likely therapeutic solutions.*

4. The psychometric approach to personality is nomothetic. Personality questionnaires describe people as being 'introverts' or 'extroverts' and 'emotionally stable' or 'emotionally unstable'. People who measure personality by using questionnaires claim that these are both reliable and valid.

4(a) [2 marks] AO1 = 2
4(b) [2 marks] AO2 = 2

(a) What is meant by the terms reliability and validity?

_____
_____
_____

(b) Outline **one** way in which the reliability **or** validity of a personality test could be assessed.

_____
_____
_____

> **Exam tip**
>
> The specification identifies 'test-retest' and 'inter observer' as ways of assessing reliability. However, it does not name specific ways of assessing validity.

5 Outline and evaluate idiographic **and** nomothetic approaches to psychological investigation.

[12 marks] AO1 = 6 AO3 = 6
[16 marks] AO1 = 6 AO3 = 10

The suggested paragraph starters below will help form your answer:

- The idiographic approach to psychological investigation focuses on… (AO1)
- It prefers to use methods that… (AO1)
- An example of the idiographic approach in psychology is… (AO1)
- The nomothetic approach to psychological investigation focuses on… (AO1)
- It prefers to use methods that… (AO1)
- An example of the nomothetic approach in psychology is… (AO1)
- One strength of the idiographic approach is that it focuses on the individual. For example, Allport… (AO3)
- However, one limitation of the idiographic approach is that it is not scientific. For example… (AO3)
- A further limitation of the idiographic approach is that its methods are relatively time consuming. For example… (AO3)
- The nomothetic approach may be better than the idiographic approach because it is able to produce general predictions about behaviour. For example… (AO3)
- An issue with both the idiographic and nomothetic approaches is that the distinction between them may be false. For example, Holt… (AO3)

Exam tip

You will need to write about both the idiographic and nomothetic approaches. If you write about only one of them, you are showing 'partial performance' and cannot be awarded full marks no matter how good your answer is.

Ethical implications of research studies and theory

Specification notes
Ethical implications of research studies and theory, including reference to social sensitivity.

Year 2 Student Book Pages 54–55

---

1 Which **one** of the following statements about the researcher's role in a psychological investigation is **false**?

Tick **one** box only.

A	The researcher has an obligation not to harm participants in a research study.	
B	The researcher must conduct a research study within strict guidelines.	
C	The researcher should treat all participants in a research study fairly.	
D	The researcher should avoid conducting research into controversial topics.	

[1 mark] AO1 = 1

---

2 A psychologist was interested in studying dispositional factors in obedience. She asked for volunteers to complete the California F-scale. One of the volunteers obtained the maximum possible score on the F-scale. At the end of the study, this volunteer asked the researcher to explain what his score on the F-scale meant.

2(a) [3 marks] AO2 = 3
2(b) [2 marks] AO2 = 2
2(c) [4 marks] AO1 = 4

(a) Using information in the item above, explain what is meant by the term 'socially sensitive research'.

Socially sensitive research is _____

_____

This research may be considered socially sensitive because _____

_____

For example, the volunteer _____

_____

> ★ **Exam tip**
> Socially sensitive research has a specific meaning in psychology, so make sure you are familiar with this and don't just answer in very general terms.

(b) Outline how ethical issues arising in this study could have been dealt with.

_____

_____

_____

(c) Apart from the research described in the item for question 2, outline **one** other socially sensitive research study **or** theory that you have studied, and explain why it is socially sensitive.

One socially sensitive research study is _____

_____

This investigated _____

_____

It is socially sensitive because _____

_____

> ★ **Exam tip**
> The question that has been asked allows you to write about a study or a theory, rather than a study and a theory.

3. A research team conducted a study into the socially sensitive area of sexual orientation. They found that a brain structure related to sexual behaviour in non-humans is significantly smaller, on average, in homosexual than in heterosexual men. A second research team attempted to replicate this finding, but found a non-significant size difference using a two-tailed test. The first research team pointed out that the second team should have used a one-tailed test, and that had they done this they would have successfully replicated the first research team's findings.

3(a)	[2 marks]	AO2 = 2
3(b)	[2 marks]	AO1 = 2
3(c)	[2 marks]	AO2 = 2

(a) Using information in the item above, explain why replication is an important feature of science.

_____

_____

_____

(b) What is the difference between a Type 1 and a Type 2 error?

_____

_____

_____

(c) Explain why the first research team believed the second research team had made a Type 2 error.

_____

_____

_____

> ⭐ **Exam tip**
>
> One of these involves incorrectly rejecting the null hypothesis, and the other involves incorrectly rejecting the experimental (alternative) hypothesis.

4. Discuss the ethical implications of research studies and theory, including reference to socially sensitive research.

| [12 marks] | AO1 = 6 | AO3 = 6 |
| [16 marks] | AO1 = 6 | AO3 = 10 |

The suggested paragraph starters below will help form your answer:

- Socially sensitive research is… (AO1)
- According to Sieber and Stanley, there are four key aspects of the research process. These are… (AO1)
- The ethical implications of research into gender development are… (AO1)
- One issue with socially sensitive research is the wider impact of the research itself. For example… (AO3)
- Another issue with socially sensitive research is that it may disadvantage marginalised groups in society. For example… (AO3)
- One issue with the current ethical guidelines is that researchers may inflict harm on a group of people. For example… (AO3)
- One solution to the issue of conducting socially sensitive research is to avoid it. For example, researchers could… (AO3)
- Another solution to the issue of conducting socially sensitive research is for researchers to engage in policy matters. For example… (AO3)

_____

_____

_____

> ⭐ **Exam tip**
>
> You can use theories and studies as evaluative material. However, remember to focus on their ethical implications rather than merely describing them.